Georges Lakhovsky

How to stay young to 100 years of age

-

The sperm therapy

Georges Lakhovsky

How to stay young to 100 years of age

-

The sperm therapy

First published 1939

*

English Translation
2021 | Jessica Düber
31135 Hildesheim | Orleans - 22

Printed Edition and Kindle Ebook by
Amazon Media EU S.à r.l., 5 Rue Plaetis,
L-2338 Luxembourg

ISBN 9798500997890

This brochure is intended exclusively for biologists,
members of the medical profession and medical students.

CHAPTER ONE

CELLULAR OSCILLATION, RESONANCE
AND THE MATERIALIZATION

All physiologists, histologists and cytologists have made an important contribution to the discovery of the various processes of life, from the formation of the first germ of the being to its death. They have described in detail the histology of the sex cells, their birth, growth, mating and the formation of the living being, but no one has ever shown us the invincible force that presides over this perpetual creation that is life. We are going to study how the sexual substances are first formed, how two complete beings materialize, each one reflecting the whole personality of the individual: the spermatozoon and the ovum. I will now show how this living matter, the source of our life, was formed. In my book "The Origin of Life", I formulated in 1926 the principle of cellular oscillation:

"Life is born of radiation,
"Sustained by radiation,
" Suppressed by any oscillatory imbalance."

This principle has been verified and confirmed over the last twelve years by numerous biological, therapeutic and clinical studies undertaken in many countries. As I have already explained cellular oscillation in detail in my various books, I will only return to it here very briefly.

The Cellular Oscillation

The cellular oscillation is the very cause of life. We know, in fact, that each living being is made up of a multitude of cells. Thus, there are no less than 200 quintillion of them in the human body.

Each living cell is a small box filled with liquid in which swim, as in a kind of aquarium, quantities of small ultramicroscopic filaments that look like tiny eels. They are called, according to their size and function, chromosomes and chondriomas. To give you an idea of their dimensions, I will tell you that the size of a cell, which varies greatly, is, on average, 15 to 20 microns (thousandths of a millimeter). The chromosomes, which are the largest of these elements, are hardly more than 5 to 6 microns long. All these anguillules, chromosomes and chondriomas, are in fact small tubes of insulating material, cholesterine, plastine, filled with a liquid, a kind of serum, containing in dissolution the mineral elements of the sea water, and conductor of electricity.

Each of these tubes constitutes an oscillating electric circuit, endowed with self-induction and capacity, analogous to a Hertz resonator.

But how can we imagine that these elementary circuits can vibrate electrically? This phenomenon is due to resonance and materialization, as I will show you.

Resonance

You know what in physics is called resonance: it is a kind of phenomenon of sympathy, which appears between two equal elements.

Thus, when in a room containing two pianos, you strike on the keyboard any note, a G for example, the other piano will instantly vibrate on the same note, G, of the same octave, to the exclusion of all other notes.

In the same way, if you hang two pendulums of the same size on the wall and make one of them swing, the other one will soon start moving and swinging at the same frequency, even if the two pendulums are separated by some meters?

This physical phenomenon is very general and has many applications. In my opinion, everything that exists in the universe is the consequence of resonance phenomena. The most striking comparison that we can find with cellular circuits is that of the T. S. F. devices. By turning the knob of one of these receivers, we adjust the circuits to the wavelength of the chosen emission, which allows us to hear, for example, a concert from Rome on 420 meters, from Paris P. T. T. on 431 meters and so on for each station that you wish to listen to.

One may wonder how chromosomes and chondriomas, as well as all the elements of the cell and of our organism, from the atom itself to the electron, can find their frequency of vibration in the surrounding environment. In order for an electric circuit to oscillate, it is essential that it finds a radiation that vibrates on its own wavelength.

Now, precisely, all the possible frequencies are found in

the immense range of vibrations, which penetrate the whole universe and which, for this reason, I have called the universion.

In a work bearing this name, I have shown that the universe is indeed filled with an immaterial substance, the vehicle of all radiations and the seat of all forces, present everywhere and in everything, and which can be considered as the cause of all that exists in the universe. It is this substance which makes atoms and electrons move as well as the stars of the firmament on their immense trajectories.

The Materialization

Now, in the universe, everything is radiation. Each matter, each substance, each being even emits a specific radiation. And, conversely, as I have explained at length in my book Matter, every radiation is susceptible of materialization.

To prove the materialization, we can invoke this classic experiment. In a glass flask or in a Petri dish, one seeds, on sterilized agar, a colony of any species of microbes: staphylococcus or colibacillus, for example. This colony of microbes, containing like any living being, most of the chemical bodies, contains, let us suppose, I millionth of milligram of iron and phosphorus. Now, after a few days, at a suitable optimum temperature, 37° C., for example, one will find in the Petri dish millions of colonies of microbes containing one million times more minerals, i.e. a few milligrams of iron and phosphorus.

Where can this iron and phosphorus come from that neither the glass nor the agar contains? They actually come from the materialization of the ambient radiations, which present radiations of all the minerals of the chemistry and of all the substances. Thus these microbes, which have developed on the agar, have materialized by resonance.

I have explained this thesis at length in numerous works, to which I would ask the reader to refer.

CHAPTER II

SPECIFIC CHARACTERISTICS OF THE GERM

I have just given you a brief overview of the essential principles of physics, biology and cell oscillation. On this triple basis, I will try to show you what life is, how it is formed, how it is born and develops, and why it disappears.

You know that everything that lives, is born one day from a germ, animal or vegetable. This is a common point in the history of all living beings. It doesn't matter what form this germ takes, nor the male and female elements whose union has created it.

In the plant, it is the fertilization of the oosphere by pollen which gives the germ which we find in the grain of wheat, in the bean, in the acorn, in the seed of the apple and in the stone of the cherry.

In animals, it is the fertilization of the female's egg by the male's spermatozoon that produces the first embryonic cell, the characteristic egg laid by the oviparous female and which develops in the womb of the viviparous female.

Why does each living being come from a well-defined germ and from this one only? Why does the germ of each animal or plant always produce a being of the same species, that is to say an absolutely specific product? Thus, a grain of wheat will always give wheat, a bean seed will always give beans.

To answer these questions, we shall first examine the conditions of the biological development of the germ. For the germ not only reproduces the species, in the biological sense of the word, but also the variety and the specific qualities. For example, a grain of hard and bearded wheat will give hard and bearded wheat. From a mirabelle stone will come a mirabelle tree which, in turn, will produce mirabelles.

I have just demonstrated that a germ always gives a specific product. But this does not mean that all the germs of the same species are identical. You know that out of the two billion men who populate the earth, no two are exactly alike. In the same way, among the countless quintillions of wheat grains harvested each year in the world, no two have exactly the same number of atoms and electrons, because these characteristic elements of the wheat grain depend on various factors: geological nature of the soil, latitude, climate and cosmic radiation that varies according to the weather.

It is the same for all the other germs of the same animal or vegetable species. So what do these specificities and diversities correspond to in each living being? To the distribution of minerals in the germ which transmits life. You know that in every living being, whether it be a microbe, a man or an elephant, a mold, a plant or a tree, we find all the bodies of chemistry in combination in mineral, ternary and nitrogenous matter. The specificity of each germ is due precisely to the proportion of mineral matter which it contains, matter which continues to materialize in the organism throughout its growth and even throughout its life, at least in theory. But in fact, as we shall see later, this materialization weakens with age due to the lack of resonance points.

To explain the admirable harmony of life, a function of the mineral distribution in the organism, I can do no better than to compare the electric radiation of the living being to the sound vibration of a great symphony orchestra. With such an orchestra, operas such as Wagner's The Master Singers, Bizet's Carmen and Puccini's Tosca can be reproduced in all their finesse and magnificence.

Let's say that, for whatever reason, the conductor of the Opera decided not to replace the failing musicians in his orchestra, either because they left or died. After a few decades, this orchestra would become progressively poorer. No doubt it would still play The Mastersingers, Carmen, and La Tosca, but the quality and beauty of these performances would also weaken, until the orchestra would come to an end.

It would be the same if the musicians, for example, violinists, cellists, harpists, pianists, etc. would not tune their instruments. The orchestra would play wrong and it would be a real cacophony. However, it is exactly the same for all living beings, including humans - and this is what interests us the most. As we age, our organism loses most of its constituent minerals, which are gradually eliminated by the wear and tear of the tissues, from about the age of forty onwards, and which can no longer materialize again in the organism because of the decrease in the oscillatory resonance points. This is the hormonal imbalance. We will see in the next chapter where this deficiency of resonance points comes from and how it can be remedied.

CHAPTER III

FUNCTION OF THE GLANDS IN OUR BODY

As you know, there are a multitude of glands in our body, whose functions are very varied, but all of which play an essential role. In general, there are five kinds of glands:

1° The excretory glands which, like the sweat glands, the kidneys, the lungs, reject toxic products harmful to the organism;

2° The digestion glands which facilitate the ingestion of food by electrolytically transforming their chemistry and distribute them in the lymph and in the blood, which carry them to the cells where they provide the necessary resonance support for the materialization of specific minerals;

3° The defense glands, which protect us against microbes, against toxins, against the variations of the ambient physical state (temperature, humidity, etc...);

4° The endocrine glands or internal secretion glands, which supply all the minerals essential to cellular oscillation and karyokinesis;

5° The sexual glands, whose secreted product is the source of our life.

Among the products secreted by these glands, some are useful, others are harmful to the organism. Those which are harmful, such as sweat, urine, carbon dioxide from the lungs and all other toxins, are expelled from the body by the excretory glands.

As for the products that are indispensable for the development of the being, they are released into the body by the endocrine glands, the digestive glands and the defense glands.

The thyroid gland secretes tyroxine; the pancreas, insulin; the adrenal glands, adrenalin; the salivary glands, saliva, whose very important role I have explained in my book Longevity (chapter: Digestion). Only two glands, which are at the source of our being, the sexual glands, secrete outside our body hormones which are indispensable to our life, and which are thus lost forever for the maintenance of the resonance points of our cellular oscillation. And this is the great tragedy of our life. This is the reason why, from the age of forty onwards, the degeneration of our organism starts to be felt. It is around this age, in fact, that the deficiencies resulting from the lack of certain minerals become apparent. The cells, no longer finding the necessary resonance points for the materialization of the minerals they lack, stop oscillating. Karyokinesis slows down, and at that moment all the pathogenic causes fall on the organism. We will look further into the origin of the evil and how it can be remedied to a certain extent.

CHAPTER IV

WHAT ARE THE SOURCES OF OUR LIFE

At the beginning of this booklet I spoke about resonance and showed that everything that exists in the universe is caused by radiation and resonance. The movement of the stars in the firmament, the dizzying rotation of the atoms in the molecule are a function of the radiation of the intermolecular space vacuum: for example, the density and weight of aluminum (13 electrons in an atom) are not the same as those of gold, which has 79 electrons in its atom. It is the intermolecular spatial vacuum that creates the specificity of each matter, of each substance: thus, any body, among the 92 elements of chemistry that we know, has its own radiation and, consequently, can materialize by resonance.

To give you an idea of the complexity and specificity of radiations, I will tell you that there are all kinds of vibrations in the universe.

Some of them directly affect our senses, such as sound vibrations and light vibrations; others, electric and ultra-sound vibrations, infra-red and ultra-violet, can only be detected and measured by appropriate devices: spectroscopes, wave meters and others.

The various vibrations differ from each other by their nature (sound waves, light waves, electric waves, etc...) and by their frequency, i.e. by their number of oscillations per second. As for electromagnetic waves, which cannot directly affect our senses, we have been able to identify them to this day by means of appropriate instruments in an enormous range of frequencies which extends from 10,000 periods per second (30,000 m. of wavelength) up to 150 quintillion periods per second (0.000002 thousandth of a millimeter of wavelength). But this upper limit of the frequencies moves back day by day as the precision of our devices increases.

However, the specificity of each living being is due to its chemical and electrical constants and, consequently, to its cellular oscillation, thus to all its vibrations. Thus, the cell of a man does not vibrate at the same frequency as the cell of a dog, a horse, a lion or an elephant.

This being said, we can explain what happens in our organism when certain minerals are missing, which leads to an oscillatory imbalance of the cells and the weakening of the materialization of these deficient minerals.

But in order to facilitate the understanding of this complex mechanism of life, we will again use the example of the opera orchestra, because the sound harmony that our ears perceive is comparable in every way to the electromagnetic harmony that escapes our senses.

We have chosen the Opera orchestra because it is the most perfect sound harmony that we know of. In such an orchestra, the distribution of all the instruments is studied with the greatest care: this is how the number of first violins was fixed at 18, that of the second violins at 16, that of the violas and cellos at 12, that of the double basses at 10, and I pass over the other instruments.

It is understandable that such a rich and varied distribution is necessary to express the soul of a drama or a lyrical tragedy through vibrations.

You know, on the other hand, that there are many other groups of instruments than the great symphonic orchestras: these are, for example, the chamber music ensembles, string or wind, which include a smaller number of instruments: trios, quartets, quintets, sextets, etc... In addition, there are a number of other instrumental associations: bands, brass bands, military bands, jazz bands, etc... Each of these groups of instruments was created to answer a determined goal and, in its kind, it can reach the perfection.

Now, as I have said above, the character of the vital functions of each being depends intimately on the distribution of all the minerals contained in its cells, which must constitute a determined vibratory harmony.

Thus, continuing our comparisons with orchestras, we can say that the vibrations of a unicellular being, of a microbe, for example, are comparable to those of a single musical instrument.

In the same way, from the vibratory point of view, the mouse is comparable to a quator, the ox to a brass band, the lion to a military band, and finally man to the orchestra of the Opera, since he is the most perfect being of the creation.

The vibrations of each being correspond to a range of radiations well determined for each living species, just as those of the various musical ensembles characterize a specific harmony for each of these ensembles.

We can now understand what happens in our organism when we pass the age of sixty. All the senile diseases arrive in caravans:

sexual deficiency, cancer, rheumatism, gout, loss of memory, etc.

Why is this so? I have already told you that our organism contains all the 92 simple bodies of chemistry, each of which has a specific vibration and whose dosage provides the specific electrical support to the cellular oscillation itself.

In our human organism, the distribution and dosage of minerals of all kinds are so perfect that the whole of its vibrations can be compared to the harmony of the opera orchestra.

Now, you know that during the same audition of the orchestra, some instruments go out of tune. Therefore, the performers have to retune their instruments after each piece of music.

Unfortunately, this is not the case for our organism, which is the best vibrating orchestra of all beings. In fact, during our lifetime, the minerals that make up our cells gradually diminish from the age of about eighteen, as we shall see later, and may even disappear in part. It is as if the instruments in an opera orchestra were out of tune and could not be retuned.

The result is a cellular oscillatory imbalance, which leads to disease and death. To restore the oscillatory balance, we would have to re-tune our cellular oscillators by providing the organism with the very substances that it lacks. Some glands are already doing this: they are the endocrine glands which secrete all kinds of substances, which are redistributed to the various tissues by the blood and by the lymph.

The only glands which, on the contrary, wear out our organism without being able to regenerate it, are the testicular glands in men and the ovarian glands in women. It is true that this loss of substance corresponds to procreation and therefore to the maintenance of the species. But, for the individual himself, this loss of substance essential to life leads fatally to degeneration and death.

Let us see how and why these losses of vital substance occur. From the time of the fertilization of the ovum by the spermatozoon until the man reaches the age of 15 to 18 years, the resonance point produced by the fertilization, and which is permanently maintained in the organism until that age, constantly ensures the materialization of all the minerals contained in the germ, the source of life.

Thus the germ continues to develop normally through cellular karyokinesis, until it reaches the perfection it attains in the adult state.

But at this precise moment two specific glands are formed, the testicles in the man, and the ovaries in the woman, which, in order to ensure procreation and the preservation of the species, stop the growth and development of the individual.

From this moment, the man having reached the peak of his form, begins to decline. His vital potential progressively decreases, at first rather weakly until about forty years of age, then more rapidly until death.

Why this decline? Because the hormonal substance, the source of life, instead of being preserved in the organism like the secretions of the other endocrine glands, is constantly exteriorized, either by ejaculation, or, even if there is no mating, in a continuous way by the urine.

The result is the weakening of the cellular oscillation, degeneration, disease and death. The same phenomenon would occur in an orchestra where the various instruments are playing out of tune, and some of them cannot play at all.

In order to remedy these degenerative processes, the organism would have to be supplied with the same chemical substances as those found in the sperm that created man.

About fifty years ago, Brown-Séquard, the father of modern opotherapy, already had the intuition of this necessity. He had the idea of administering to man a drug extracted from the testicular glands of animals. The idea was a good one, but it was not followed up because of a lack of specificity, and this is essential. It would be better to replace the deficient instruments of a symphony orchestra by those of a jazz or military band.

Voronoff went further and got closer to the truth. He tried to graft onto the testicle of man fragments of chimpanzee testicles, whose physiology is the closest to ours. He thought, like Brown-Séquard, that in this way the activity of the reproductive functions and even that of all the other glands would be reinforced in man.

Indeed, it was found that the transplantation of monkey glands activated the sexual functions of man for a certain period of time (3 or 4 years). But, in spite of the very close relationship between the monkey and the man, there is no identity between his glands and ours, therefore insufficient specificity.

I thought that in order to obtain the best and long-lasting results, it would be necessary to introduce into our organism exactly the same specific substances as those which have provided our life with the sperm or the ovum, which amounts to the same thing.

So let us find out what this ideal promatter of our

organism, the sperm, is, how it is produced and what essential role it plays in our existence.

You know that our testicles contain numerous epithelial canaliculi. The walls of these ductules, which lead to the urethra, are lined with small fins that look like a radiator. It is these canaliculi which secrete, between these fins, a spermatic substance, which is the richest in minerals of all the substances contained in our organism.

Besides albuminoids, protein substances of all kinds, and various organic salts: phosphates, chlorides, sulfates, etc., this substance contains all the minerals of chemistry: sodium, magnesium, calcium, etc., and even traces of gold and platinum. But why is this substance the cause of life, contrary to the secretions of the other glands of the body? It is because the richness of these minerals and their distribution are such that when two cells (sperm and egg), containing all these substances, combine, an appropriate radiation and resonance is produced, which causes karyokinesis, that is, cell division, the process of which you know, to create a perfect being, which at its birth will already be a man. So it is because of the wonderful distribution of all these minerals that life is created. It follows that the combination of all these minerals to form the spermatic substance is really the cause of our life.

The same is obviously true of the egg, which is the partner of the spermatozoon. The chemical analyses which have been made of the testicular substance and the ovarian substance have shown, indeed, that the chemism of these two substances is exactly the same.

We can now understand how life develops and is

maintained in its entirety until adulthood, but why the decline begins from that moment on, why we wither and eventually die.

I explained to you at the beginning of this work that the development of every living being is a consequence of materialization.

I have succeeded, with my multi-wave oscillator, in accelerating the cellular oscillation and, consequently, the materialization of the minerals rarefied in the organism by the demineralization of the tissues. However, this process can only work if there are still some traces of organic substances necessary for karyokinesis and which can serve as resonance points for materialization. It goes without saying that if these resonance points are missing, no materialization is possible, just as in a well sterilized Petri dish, no microbe will develop if it has not been previously seeded, forming a resonance point. This is the drama of our existence!

To remedy the deficiency of the resonance points I thought that if we could provide the organism with a supplement of these deficient spermatic minerals, so wonderfully distributed and which are the source of all life, we would succeed in re-establishing not only the oscillatory equilibrium, but also the perfection and suppleness which characterized all our tissues during our youth, when the substances were in abundance.

In this way we would eliminate senility and all the illnesses which derive from it.

Pathogenic causes of all kinds would disappear and we would be able to extend our life to unsuspected limits: perhaps a few hundred years. Unfortunately, it is obviously very difficult to obtain this substance. So I thought long and hard about this problem, the solution of which could, in my opinion, save humanity from much suffering.

After a thousand reflections, I looked for a practical way to obtain this spermatic substance. Of course, it was out of the question to ask every man to collect this liquid after ejaculation.

Finally, an idea came to me. I thought that this raw material of life could be obtained in the so-called "houses of tolerance" where it is produced in large quantities. In these establishments one could obtain a sufficient quantity of it not only for experiments, but also to improve the whole human race. Now it is possible to collect spermatic liquid in the best conditions of hygiene and cleanliness. Indeed, the young men of twenty to thirty years of age who frequent these houses generally use condoms. As the substance is thus enclosed, after ejaculation, in an aseptic envelope, nothing is easier than to transfer the contents into a jar half-filled with 96° alcohol, which ensures its immediate sterilization.

There is nothing to fear, under these conditions, of the risks of contagion by germs of any kind (syphilis, gonorrhoea, etc...) since this spermatic material, being used only after having remained several weeks in alcohol, is obviously free of any pathogenic microbe.

It is therefore safe to use this substance in the form of drops taken by mouth, or better still by intramuscular or testicular injections. Let us add that the spermatic matter thus collected is all the more healthy and specific as it comes from young people who use condoms precisely to avoid any risk of contagion.

One could fear that some people would feel a real disgust at the thought of absorbing a drug of this origin. This is wrong, because the drug, once chemically treated, is no longer the same substance. I have succeeded, by extracting the minerals, in ridding this substance of all the woody, cellulosic and other precipitating matter, and in preserving only the soluble mineral substances so as to obtain a transparent, odorless and tasteless liquid, which obviously cannot arouse any repugnance. Moreover, it does not contain any toxic principle whatsoever, since it is the human organic product par excellence, source of our life.

There are, moreover, medical treatments that are much dirtier in reality. You know that at present, in order to cure certain acute furunculosis, serums made from the pus of the abscesses of the most seriously affected patients are injected. This spermatic substance is therefore much less repulsive, much safer than all the serums based on microbes or on glands from animal corpses, as is the case for opotherapy.

So I easily obtained this substance. Once in possession of this admirable liquid, I had to experiment with it: but how to go about it?

It is a given in microbiology, as in biology, that any experiment must first be attempted on animals, generally on guinea pigs, mice, dogs, etc...

But, in this case, this method is not indicated, and even goes against the goal. This new procedure is based on the specificity of the human sperm substance. It is therefore conceivable that by experimenting with this specific human substance on animals, one could only obtain a negative or mediocre result, as if, following the Brown-Séquard method, one applied the glandular secretions of animals to man in reverse.

My first idea was therefore to experiment on myself, because, in all the research I have done up to now, I have always considered myself as a guinea pig and offered myself as a subject of experiment. This is the best way for a researcher to proceed: there is nothing like observing oneself in every detail to verify the validity of one's experiments.

It would therefore be a heresy and the experiment would be a failure in advance if the effect of this spermatic substance were to be tested on animals, even those close to man, such as monkeys, since in this case, the essential aspect of this new therapy is the specificity which would not be respected in this case. However, after reflection, I said to myself that my case would probably not be very convincing, because, for more than fourteen years that I have been wearing my oscillating circuits, that I have been influenced almost daily by the radiation of my multi-wave device and that I sometimes treat myself with this oscillator, my health is such that, in spite of my age (69 years), I still do not feel any symptom of senility, whatever it may be. And yet, as I said in my book "Longevity", I was so seriously ill twenty-seven years ago that I was condemned by all the medical authorities. On the other hand, I now feel such vigor, such euphoria, that, in spite of my sixty-nine years of age, I am barely fifty.

Is not the best barometer of my health the considerable amount of work I do daily (nearly 18 hours a day) without the least fatigue? And if this new medicine can act favorably on the body, as I am convinced, I really don't see what I could do better for myself. However, I thought it would be useful to offer myself as a guinea pig, by first trying this treatment on myself, not to reinforce my health level, which I did not need, but especially to check if there were no contraindications in this application.

So I began to take 4 to 6 drops of this liquor in half a glass of water at each meal. I observed myself attentively, with the intention of suspending this treatment as soon as I noticed the slightest pathological disorder.

However, it is precisely the opposite that happened, since my health, which was already excellent, improved again.

So I continued these experiments on myself for about a month and a half. Almost every day I felt certain strengths coming back, certain sensations of youth that I had not felt with such vigor for forty years. Wanting to test my new youthful strength, I ran after a bus in full march and I managed to catch it after a race of a hundred meters, without the slightest breathlessness, which I could never have done before.

But what confirms my observations is the fact that all the people who haven't seen me for a few months or a few years testify to their astonishment and their surprise to find me so rejuvenated.

Now sure of the harmlessness of the process, I did not hesitate to experiment it on a certain number of friends, old men from sixty-five to seventy-five years of age, suffering from senility and in full degeneration, who therefore had everything to gain and nothing to lose.

The results I obtained exceeded all my expectations. Most of the subjects experience, thanks to the daily absorption of this substance, a rejuvenation that it has never been possible to obtain until now, neither by grafting, nor by any other opotherapeutic treatment.

It is with enthusiasm that I report these facts of experience to the medical profession, to biologists and to scientists throughout the world.

However, one should not believe that one automatically obtains these beneficial effects on any subject with any dose. Thus, out of ten people on whom I tried this treatment, six had a positive result; for the other four, the result was null or even sometimes negative, causing some organic disorders.

But I did not lose heart, I thought that it was a question of dosage. During this talk, I compared our body to a symphony orchestra that gives the most perfect vibratory harmony. If certain instruments, violins, cellos, harps, pianos, go out of tune, it is not a matter of turning the key anyhow, in any direction. On the contrary, the string must be stretched to the precise point where. it resonates with the pitch. The same is true for the symphony orchestra made up of all the cells in the human body.

But how can we tune our organism by means of the spermatic fluid? Well, I have managed to find a rational solution to this difficult problem. It is simply with the help of the pendulum of dowsing, which allows to tune exactly the dose of liquid in resonance with the organism of each individual.

At these words, I see immediately rising up against this method, the numerous men of science who do not believe in dowsing, under the pretext that this art has not been explained scientifically yet.

However, although I am not a dowser myself, I have witnessed such extraordinary experiences that for me no doubt is allowed and that the undeniable facts of experience have led to my absolute conviction. I then looked for the scientific explanation of these phenomena, and I exposed it in several of my works, notably Eternity, Life and My, Earth and Us and especially Matter.

My explanations have been adopted by most radiesthesists and even by practitioners who treat patients by radiesthesic methods.

Thus Abbé Mermet, the reverend father Wehrmeister from Munich, the famous pendulum-maker Haardt from Zurich and many others, have practiced dowsing according to my theories. But what gave me the greatest pleasure was to receive the confirmation of my theory by an eminent Belgian scientist, Dr. Derenne, Perpetual Secretary of the Royal Academy of Sciences of Belgium. In an article published in the magazine "Le Radiesthésiste de Liège" in December 1938, Dr. Derenne, after having spoken about the radiations of the human body which can be captured and measured, expresses himself as follows:

"Here is an example: Called upon, two weeks ago, to examine a patient in the company of an eminent Belgian pendulist, I found myself in the presence of a young man whose external appearance did not allow me to prejudge the illness from which he was suffering. Without asking the slightest question to the patient, whom neither of us had ever seen, the dowser carried out his examination and wrote down his conclusions. In my turn, I proceeded to meticulous clinical investigations and diagnosed progressive türberculosis of the left lung, intestinal disorders of bacillary origin with tuberculous ulceration of the rectal mucosa. Only then was the radiesthesia form submitted to me. It read: tuberculosis of the left lung, disorders of the small intestine, lesion of the rectum.

"This disturbing example has nothing supernatural about it and is far from being isolated. It must therefore be admitted that the sick organ not only radiates, but also does so differently from the healthy organ.

"To explain the origin of the waves, whether they emanate from the living or the inanimate world, as well as their translation by the pendulum, a number of more or less plausible hypotheses have been proposed. The one that seems to me the most well-founded is exposed by the learned physicist M. Lakhovsky in his book La Matière.

"Each atom produces a specific compression within the ether, which translates into radiation at specific wavelengths, characteristic of the substance in question. These characteristic rays propagate throughout the universe, pass through our body and create a field of influence there, which is combined with the radiation from the center of the oscillating cellular elements chromosomes and chondriomas. This resulting field creates a new oscillatory state in the cells of our body, which in turn is reflected in the movements of the pendulum. "

"These, in the opinion of most scholars, have a physical origin, that is, they are due to weak unconscious and involuntary muscle contractions, controlled by the autonomic nervous system. They do not have their origin in the brain of the experimenter who would order the pendulum to perform, according to his will, gyrations, ellipses, beats, in such and such a direction or in such and such a number. The dowser, on the contrary, must have an indifferent mind and above all not want to find.

Just like a T.S.F. receiver, he must tune himself to the thing sought by eliminating the crowd of waves that surround him and by tuning his nervous system to the reception of the only desirable radiation."

I will now explain how we manage to tune the exact dose of spermatic fluid to tune in resonance the symphony orchestra that is our body.

I therefore turned to one of the aces of medical radiesthesia, Doctor E. B., former head of clinic in Paris. Having come to my laboratory, he proved to me that this tuning is very easy to do. It is enough for him to take a letter or even simply the signature of a subject, to put on this signature a small bottle of spermatic liquid and to prospect the whole thing by means of the pendulum, asking himself by thought about the number of drops to prescribe.

Naturally, the result is even more reliable if the subject holds a small tube of this liquid in his hand, over which the pendulum moves. The pendulum then starts spinning, precisely for the number of drops that should be ordered to the subject in order to bring his organism into resonance.

Thus, within a few minutes, he managed to find the number of drops corresponding to five different subjects. I could not believe my eyes when I saw this childishly simple technique. As I expressed my astonishment to Dr. B., he told me: "It is not difficult and you can do it yourself. "I tried it and I immediately obtained the same result as him, although I was not a dowser.

Nevertheless, deep inside me there was still some skepticism. I tried, however, by giving each of these subjects the prescribed number of drops. Well, I noticed that after about ten days my subjects all came to me to express their gratitude for the positive results they had obtained. Here is the infallible way to re-tune the symphonic orchestra of our body when its vibrations are out of tune. This treatment is all the more remarkable because it is not a matter of recommending a patent or any pharmaceutical speciality. Any biologist, any doctor can, in fact, obtain this material very easily, as I said above. Naturally, I shared this discovery and the progress of these experiments with a certain number of scientists and with my friends, the heads of the Pasteur Institute. Most of them were very enthusiastic about this method and this discovery. One of them even said to me, "This is a considerable event in the history of biology, the consequences of which could be incalculable. "

Most said to me:

"We understand very well that you have undertaken your experiments on yourself first and then on other men, since it is a question of the specificity of the human species.

"But you are going to experience considerable difficulties in having your method admitted by official science, since you are going off the beaten track and you want to apply to man a method that has not been previously tested on animals."

"We know that you are revolutionary, but that is no reason for us to listen to you!" I answered by protesting that I am not revolutionary, that I am used to saying things as I think and as I see them, even at the risk of displeasing some ignorant "scholars". Besides, my experiences have proved me right.

I am firmly convinced - and my research confirms this point of view every day - that this method will easily cure the most serious diseases, such as tuberculosis, syphilis and even cancer. For all diseases are caused by the cellular oscillatory imbalance produced by the deficiency of hormonal substances, sources of life, in certain tissues and organs.

In fact, in biology and medicine, everyone agrees that it is the resistance of our organism that allows us to fight victoriously against all diseases. We have millions of microbes in our mouths, in our lungs, in our intestines and our nasal cavities are real biological ovens where microbes develop in considerable quantities.

If all these microbes had a hold on our organism, humanity would have disappeared a long time ago. It is therefore the resistance of this organism which kills the microbes and eliminates all pathogenic causes. But to have this beautiful resistance, it is necessary that all the glands secrete normally and it is with the spermatic matter of the man that one must arrive at this beautiful result.

Undoubtedly, the "moralists" will revolt at the thought that one should turn to such houses of tolerance to save the human race.

I do not intend to enter into a moral discussion here, which has no place in this booklet and which is not within my competence. I will only say that if the law authorizes these establishments, it is because it considers that they probably serve a social purpose.

But in this case, I am convinced that if their usefulness is debatable at present, it will certainly not be tomorrow, when the method I propose will have been applied to save millions of our fellow men from the most serious diseases and to prolong human life without suffering. These houses will no longer be "of tolerance", but of public utility.

Let us even admit - and I will gladly agree on this point - that these houses constitute an offense to morality and religion. Moreover, I would be tempted to oppose their creation, if they did not exist. But since they do exist, we might as well take advantage of the precious substance they can provide for the greater good of humanity. I am convinced that later on, in the future, these houses will no longer be considered as places of shame and forbidden pleasures, but as annexes to the laboratories of the Faculty of Medicine.

Now that I have explained to you the way to improve our vital balance and to postpone death to unsuspected limits, we can ask ourselves if life is really worth being prolonged to this point.

Indeed, we are currently witnessing atrocious spectacles. It really seems that man has lost his reason and even his sense of civilization.

The whole world is in turmoil: on all sides, there are nothing but revolutions, civil and foreign wars, complete destruction of cities, artistic and historical monuments, massacres of defenseless populations, and, it must be said, also on the part of those who claim to act in the name of civilization: bombing of open cities under the pretext of achieving military objectives. Thousands and tens of thousands of children, women and old people have been massacred, innocent victims of these absurd killings. Our globe has become the scene of merciless ideological struggles and great nations are governed by gangsters. Whether their name is Stalin, Hitler or Mussolini, their methods of coercion and their bloodthirsty sentiments are the same. They murder and martyr some in the name of the proletariat, others in the name of racism. For them, every treaty is a rag, every word given is worthless. Their doctrine is the law of the strongest, which they exercise through cowardice over the weakest.

However, I believe that man has a biological, social and moral role to play in this world. In spite of the madness and the imbalance of certain brains which, by combining their forces, make terrible ravages, I estimate that the great majority of the men is still impregnated with the moral and civilizing virtues which humanity took so long to acquire and which it bought so dearly. And that is why I have resolved to publish this new therapy. I am convinced that it will make it possible to prolong life in order to compensate for the cruel losses that the human race is currently suffering because of the unleashing of savagery. I do this all the more willingly because I would not forgive myself for taking the secret of this process to the grave.

For we live in such an unbalanced age, where life is so constantly threatened, that the healthiest man, physically and morally, is never sure of tomorrow. Moreover, my function as a guinea pig in all my experiments exposes my life to a perpetual danger. I bequeath to humanity this method which I advocate to save it. And this is, at the same time, my scientific and moral testament. May the civilized world benefit from it and make the best use of it.

Made in the USA
Middletown, DE
11 August 2024

58926039R00020